# READING/WRITING
# COMPANION

Mc
Graw
Hill
Education

**Cover:** Nathan Love, Erwin Madrid

mheducation.com/prek-12

Send all inquiries to:
McGraw-Hill Education
Two Penn Plaza
New York, NY 10121

ISBN: 978-0-07-901842-7
MHID: 0-07-901842-4

Printed in the United States of America.

8 9 10 11 12 13  SWI  27 26 25 24 23 22            C

# Welcome to Wonders!

Explore exciting Literature, Science, and Social Studies texts!

★ READ about the world around you!

★ THINK, SPEAK, and WRITE about genres!

★ COLLABORATE in discussions and inquiry!

★ EXPRESS yourself!

**my.mheducation.com**

Use your student login to read texts and practice phonics, spelling, grammar, and more!

# Unit 1 Take a New Step

## Start Smart

## The Big Idea
**What can we learn when we try new things?**

# Week 1 • Make New Friends

# Week 2 • Get Up and Go!

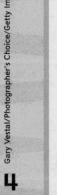

# Week 3 • Use Your Senses

# We Are All Readers

**Talk** about what the children are reading.

 **Draw** what you like to read about.

# We Are All Writers

**Talk** about what the children are writing.

 **Draw** one thing you did this summer.

 **Write** your name.

**Essential Question**

## How is everyone special?

**Talk** about what the children are doing.

 **Draw** one thing you like to do.

**Talk** about the story.
How is the gray duckling different?

 **Draw** how this duckling is different.

**Listen** to part of the story.

 **Talk** about the direction
Mother Duck gives her ducklings.

 **Say** the directions below in order.
Then act them out.

- **Stand up.**
- **Hop.**
- **Sit down.**

**Find Text Evidence**

 Read to find out what makes the children special.

 Circle the letters **A** and **a**.

# I Am Special!

 **Find Text Evidence**

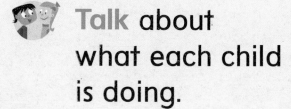 **Talk** about what each child is doing.

**Circle** the child who is playing with the balls.

# Shared Read

 Find Text Evidence

 **Talk** about what the girl on this page is doing.

 **Retell** the story. Use the pictures to help you.

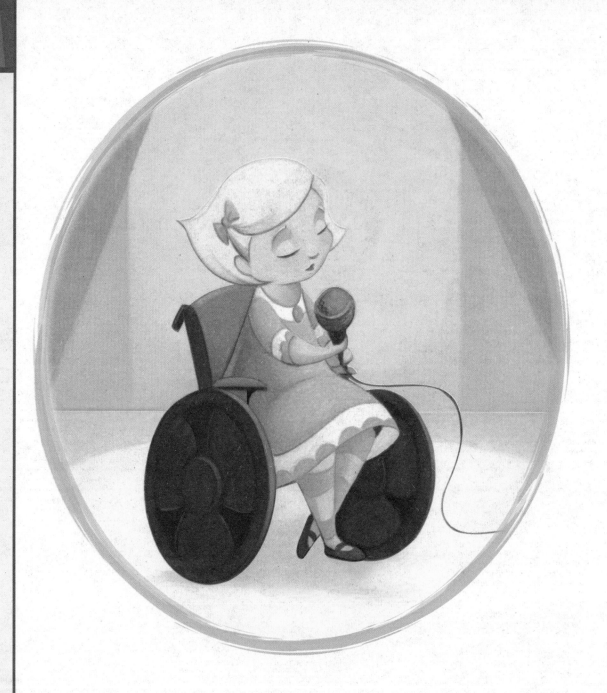

The End!

## I Am Special

 **Draw** a picture of yourself.

 **Write** your name.

Hello! My name is

_____

- - - - - - - - - - - - - - - - - - - - - - - - - - -

_____

**Draw** what makes you special.

 **Say** hello and introduce yourself.

 **Share** your work.

**Find Text Evidence**

Read to find out what each child does.

Circle and read aloud the word **I**.

# Look at Me!

Liza McCorkle/Vetta/Getty Images

I .

jump

🔍 **Find Text Evidence**

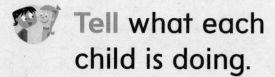 **Tell** what each child is doing.

🖍️ **Circle** what the girl needs to help her paint.

I  .

dance

Ariel Skelley/Blend Images

I  paint.

## 🔍 Find Text Evidence

**Circle** the child who is writing.

**Retell** the text. Use the words and photos to help you.

I  .

read

I .
write

# Talk About It

**Talk** about what the family is doing.

 **Draw** one thing you do with your family.

**Talk** about the story.
What do the mice do?

**Draw** an important part of the story.

**Listen** to part of the story.

 **Talk** about what the mice need.

 **Write** about one thing you may need in school. Then tell your teacher.

I may need

_____

- - - - - - - - - - - - - - - - - - - - - - - - - - - - - - - - - - -

_____

- - - - - - - - - - - - - - - - - - - - - - - - - - - - - - - - - - -

_____

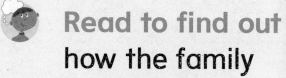
**Find Text Evidence**

 Read to find out how the family is having fun.

Look at the picture. Tell what each person is doing.

# Family Fun!

**Find Text Evidence**

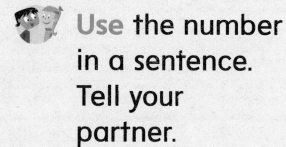 **Circle** the people at the table. Then count the people.

**Use** the number in a sentence. Tell your partner.

# Shared Read

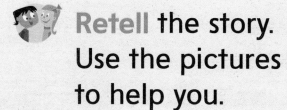 **Circle** the person the cake is for. How do you know?

**Retell** the story. Use the pictures to help you.

## My Family and Me

 Draw a picture of you and your family.

**Draw** a place you go with your family.

 **Say** hello and introduce yourself.

 **Share** your work.

**Find Text Evidence**

Read to find out what the family is doing.

Circle what the boy can pour. Use the picture to help you know what the word **pour** means. Then tell your partner what **pour** means.

# Fun Together!

I can .

pour

 **Find Text Evidence**

**Tell** what the family is making. Use the pictures to help you.

**Circle** and read aloud the word **can**.

I can  .

mix

I can  .

bake

# Shared Read

 **Find Text Evidence**

**Circle** what the girl can eat. How do you know?

**Retell** the story. Use the words and pictures to help you.

I can clean .

I can  !

eat

# Talk About It

**Talk** about what the girl can do.

 **Draw** one thing you can do.

**Talk** about the text.
What can the children do?

**Draw** one thing they can do.

**Listen** to part of the text.

 **Talk** about what you would like to learn this year. Now listen to what your partner wants to learn.

 **Draw** what you would like to learn.

**Find Text Evidence**

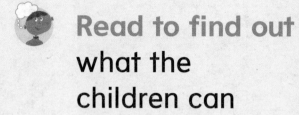 Read to find out what the children can do at school.

Circle the letter **S**.

# At School

**Find Text Evidence**

 **Think** about how the children on this page can take turns talking.

**Tell** your ideas to your partner. Take turns talking.

Today

Aa

# Shared Read

**Talk** about what the children are doing on these pages.

**Retell** the story. Use the pictures to help you.

## I Can!

 **Draw** one thing you can do at school.

**Draw** one thing you can do at home.

 **Say** hello and introduce yourself.

 **Share** your work.

 Read to find out what each child can do.

 Listen to the words in the title. Clap for each word.

# What Can I Do?

I can .
ride

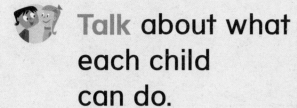

**Find Text Evidence**

**Talk** about what each child can do.

**Circle** and read aloud the words **I** and **can**.

I can .
rake

LWA/Dann Tardif/Blend Images/Getty Images

I can .
walk

**Find Text Evidence**

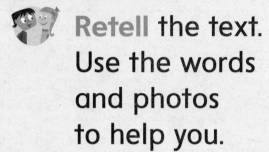

**Circle** what each child likes to read.

**Retell** the text. Use the words and photos to help you.

Can I 📖 ?

read

Henglein and Steets/age fotostock

I can !
read

# Unit 1
# Take a New Step

## The Big Idea

What can we learn when we try new things?

 **Say** hello to your partner and say your name.

 **Talk** about each photo.

 **Circle** someone in each photo who is trying something new.

# Talk About It

**Essential Question** How can we get along with new friends?

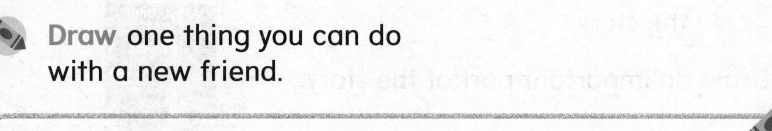

**Talk** about what these friends are doing.

**Draw** one thing you can do with a new friend.

Retell the story.

Draw an important part of the story.

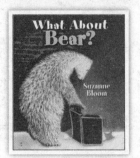

Text Evidence

Page

**Talk** about ways friends can get along.

 **Draw** one way friends can get along.

**Key details tell information that helps you understand the story.**

 Listen to part of the story.

 Talk about key details.

 Write one key detail.

One key detail is

_____

_____

_____

_____

**Draw** the detail you wrote about.

 **Look** at pages 18–19 and 32–33.

 **Talk** about how Bear's feelings change.

 **Write** and **draw** your ideas.

First Bear feels

Then Bear feels

_____

- - - - - - - - - - - - - - - - - - - - - - - - - - - - - - - -

_____

**Find Text Evidence**

 Read to find out what the boy can do.

 Read and point to each word in the title.

# I Can

I can  the .

see    mitt

 **Find Text Evidence**

 **Underline** the word **the**.

 **Circle** an object whose name begins with the same sound as **map**.

I can 👁 the 🧹.

see        mop

I can  see the  drum .

# Shared Read

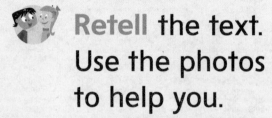

**Circle** the things whose name begins with the same sound as **map**.

**Retell** the text. Use the photos to help you.

I can 👁 the ⦾.

see　　　marbles

I can the .

see                    broom

**Look** at the photographs.
What are some ways to be a friend?

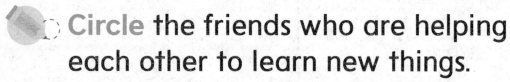 **Circle** the friends who are helping
each other to learn new things.

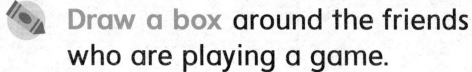 **Draw a box** around the friends
who are playing a game.

**Listen** to the list.

 **Talk** about the directions on the list. When can you use these directions to make a new friend?

1. Say hello.
2. Tell your name.
3. Ask your new friend to play.

 **Say** the directions on the list in order.

 **Act** out the directions. Take turns with a partner.

---

**Quick Tip**

A **list** is a quick way to give information.

Each item is on its own line.

**Talk About It**

How do the photographs in this text show ways to be friends?

**Find Text Evidence**

Read to find out what the girl can do.

Circle an object whose name begins with the same sound as **mop**.

Can I see the map?

**Find Text Evidence**

Underline the uppercase letters.

Circle the word the.

I can.

Can I 👁️ the 🪑 ?
see        chair

**Find Text Evidence**

Circle what the girl can see on page 86.

Retell the story. Use the pictures to help you.

I can.

I can 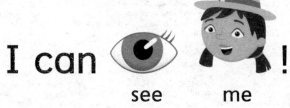 !

see    me

# How to Be a Good Friend

**Step 1** **Talk** about how to be a good friend.

**Step 2** **Write** a question about what a good friend might do.

_____

- - - - - - - - - - - - - - - - - - - - - - - - - - - - - -

_____

- - - - - - - - - - - - - - - - - - - - - - - - - - - - - -

_____

**Step 3** **Talk** to classmates. Ask them your question.

**Step 4** Draw what you learned.

**Step 5** Choose a good way to present your work.

**Talk** about what the friends in the art are doing.

 **Compare** these friends to the friends in *What About Bear?*

**Quick Tip**

We can **compare** things. We can ask:

*How are things alike?*

*How are things different?*

# What I Know Now

Think about the texts you read this week.

The texts tell about

_____

- - - - - - - - - - - - - - - - - - - - - - - - - - - - - - - - - -

_____

_____

- - - - - - - - - - - - - - - - - - - - - - - - - - - - - - - - - -

_____

 **Think** about what you learned this week.
What else would you like to learn?
Talk about your ideas.

 **Share** one thing you learned
about fiction stories.

# Talk About It

**Talk** about how these baby penguins move.

 **Draw** how your favorite animal moves.

Sue Flood/Stone/Getty Images

**Retell** the story.

**Draw** an important part of the story.

**Text Evidence**

Page

**Talk** about how the animals in *Pouch!* move.

 **Draw** how one of the animals moves.

The text and pictures in a story give key details. Key details tell information that helps you understand the story.

 **Listen** to part of the story.

 **Talk** about key details.

 **Write** one key detail.

One key detail is

_____

- - - - - - - - - - - - - - - - - - - - - - - - -

_____

_____

- - - - - - - - - - - - - - - - - - - - - - - - -

_____

**Draw** the detail you wrote about.

 **Look** at page 12. How does the author let you know that Joey is talking?

 **Draw** and **write** what Joey wants to do when he says, "Pouch!"

Joey wants to

_____

- - - - - - - - - - - - - - - - - - -

_____

**Look** at page 34.

 **Talk** about what the baby kangaroos mean when they say, "No, thanks."

 **Draw** what the baby kangaroos want to do.

🔍 **Find Text Evidence**

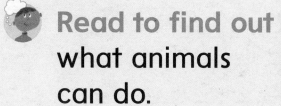 **Read to find out** what animals can do.

✏️ **Circle** the word **We**.

# We Can

Eastphoto/age fotostock

We can  .

walk

**Find Text Evidence**

 **Ask** questions you may have about the text as you read. This can help you learn information.

**Circle** animals that can hop.

We can 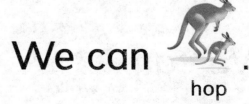 .

hop

We can  .

climb

# Shared Read

🔍 **Find Text Evidence**

**Underline** words that have the same middle sound as fan.

**Retell** the text. Use the photos to help you.

We can 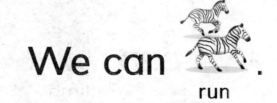.
run

(t) Alan Carey/Corbis; (b) Nancy Carlson

We can .

hug

**Look** at the photos on pages 106–107. How do different baby animals move?

Mother lion and cubs

Mother duck and ducklings

**Circle** the baby animals that are swimming.

**Draw a box** around the baby animals that are crawling.

**Quick Tip**

We can look for **clues**, or details, in photos to learn about ways baby animals move.

Mother horse and foal

Baby turtles

 **Talk** about how the photos give information about ways baby animals move.

**Talk About It**

Titles give information about what a text is about. How does the title, "Baby Animals on the Move!" help you know what this text is about?

**Find Text Evidence**

Read to find out what the animals can do.

Underline the lowercase letters in the title.

# I Can, We Can

I can  .

swim

# Shared Read

🔍 **Find Text Evidence**

✏️ **Underline** the word **We**.

✏️ **Circle** animals that are in the water.

We can ___.

swim

I can  .

fly

**Circle** words that have the same middle sound as **bat**.

**Retell** the story. Use the pictures to help you.

We can .

fly

We can .

run

# How a Baby Animal Moves

**Step 1** Talk about ways baby animals move. Choose one to learn about.

**Step 2** Write a question about how the animal moves.

_____

- - - - - - - - - - - - - - - - - - - - - - - - - - - -

_____

_____

- - - - - - - - - - - - - - - - - - - - - - - - - - - -

_____

**Step 3** Look at books or use the Internet.

**Step 4** Draw what you learned.

**Step 5** Choose a good way to present your work.

# The Little Bird

I saw a little bird
Come hop, hop, hop.
So I called, "Little bird,
Will you stop, stop, stop?"

I asked the little bird,
"How do you do?"
But it shook its little tail,
And far away it flew.

 **Listen** to the poem.

 **Think** about how the little bird moves.

 **Compare** how the little bird moves with the way Joey moves in *Pouch!*

**Quick Tip**

To talk about baby animals, we can say:

*The little bird can ____.*

*Joey can ____.*

# What I Know Now

Think about the texts you read this week.

The texts tell about

_____

- - - - - - - - - - - - - - - - - -

_____

- - - - - - - - - - - - - - - - - -

_____

 **Think** about what you learned this week.
What else would you like to learn?
Talk about your ideas.

 **Share** one thing you learned
about fiction stories.

# Talk About It

Essential Question **How can your senses help you learn?**

**Talk** about how this girl uses her senses.

 **Draw** one way you use your senses.

**Retell** the text.

**Draw** a fact from the text.

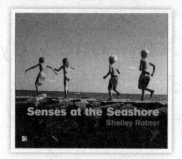

Senses at the Seashore
Shelley Rotner

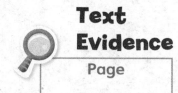

Text Evidence

Page

**Talk** about ways people use their senses.

 **Draw** one way that people use their senses.

**Nonfiction includes facts and key details.**
**Key details tell information about the topic.**

 **Listen** to part of the text.

 **Talk** about key details.

 **Write** one key detail.

One key detail is

_____

- - - - - - - - - - - - - - - - - - - - - - - -

_____

_____

- - - - - - - - - - - - - - - - - - - - - - - -

_____

**Draw** the detail you wrote about.

**Listen** to parts of the text.

 **Talk** about how your senses help you know what the seashore is like.

 **Draw** details here.

|  see | |
| --- | --- |
|  hear | |

**Look** at pages 24–25.

 **Talk** about how the words and photos help you know about seaweed.

 **Draw** and **write** about seaweed.

The seaweed is

🔍 **Find Text Evidence**

👧 **Read to find out** what Sam can see.

✏️ **Circle** words that begin with the same sound as **sun.**

# Sam Can See

We can see Sam.

# Shared Read

🔍 **Find Text Evidence**

✏️ **Underline** the word **see.**

✏️ **Circle** what Sam can see.

We can see the 🐦.

bird

Sam can see the .
bird

**Find Text Evidence**

 **Ask** questions you may have about the story.

 **Retell** the story. Use the pictures to help you.

Sam can see the  .

bird

The  **bird** can see Sam.

**Listen** to the poems. Look at the pictures. How do we use our senses to learn?

 **Circle** what the girl can smell.

 **Draw a box** around what the woman can taste.

**Quick Tip**

We can talk about senses using these words:

*We can smell ____.*

*We can taste ____.*

**Listen** to "I Smell Springtime" again.

 **Talk** about words the author uses in the poem that tell spring is here.

 **Draw** one way the poem tells that spring is here.

**Talk About It**

Why are "I Smell Springtime" and "Taste of Purple" good titles for these poems?

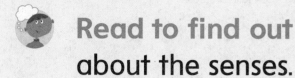
🔍 **Find Text Evidence**

Read to find out about the senses.

✏️ **Circle** the word **see**.

# I Can See

Anne Ackermann/Taxi/Getty Images

I can see the 🍎.

apple

🔍 **Find Text Evidence**

✏️ **Circle** things whose name begins with the same sound as **am**.

✏️ **Underline** the word **can**.

I can .

touch

I can  smell .

### Find Text Evidence

Circle what helps the girl taste.

Retell the text. Use the photos to help you.

I can .

hear

I can .
taste

# Research a Sense

**Step 1** Talk about your senses.
Choose one to learn about.

**Step 2** Write a question about this sense.

_____

- - - - - - - - - - - - - - - - - - -

_____

- - - - - - - - - - - - - - - - - - -

_____

**Step 3** Look at books or use the Internet.

**Step 4** Draw what you learned.

**Step 5** Choose a good way to present your work.

**Talk** about how your senses can help you learn about flowers like these.

 **Think** about what you learned in *Senses at the Seashore*.

 **Compare** how your senses can help you learn about flowers and the seashore.

**Quick Tip**

Our senses help us tell how things are alike and different.

Rijksmuseum, Amsterdam

# What I Know Now

Think about the texts you read this week.

The texts tell about

_____

- - - - - - - - - - - - - - - - - - - -

_____

- - - - - - - - - - - - - - - - - - - -

_____

 **Think** about what you learned this week.
What else would you like to learn?
Talk about your ideas.

 **Share** one thing you learned
about nonfiction texts.

# My Sound-Spellings

| | | | | | | |
|---|---|---|---|---|---|---|
| **Aa** a — apple | **Bb** b — bat | **Cc** c ck k — camel | **Dd** d — dolphin | **Ee** e — egg | **Ff** f — fire | **Gg** g — guitar |
| **Hh** h_ — hippo | **Ii** i — insect | **Jj** j — jump | **Kk** c k ck — koala | **Ll** l — lemon | **Mm** m — map | **Nn** n — nest |
| **Oo** o — octopus | **Pp** p — piano | **Qq** qu_ — queen | **Rr** r — rose | **Ss** s — sun | **Tt** t — turtle | **Uu** u — umbrella |
| **Vv** v — volcano | **Ww** w_ — window | **Xx** x — box | **Yy** y_ — yo-yo | **Zz** z _s — zipper | | |

Aa Bb Cc Dd Ee

Ff Gg Hh Ii Jj

Kk Ll Mm Nn

Oo Pp Qq Rr

Ss Tt Uu Vv

Ww Xx Yy Zz